How does it feel?

Bobbie Kalman

Crabtree Publishing Company

www.crabtreebooks.com

Created by Bobbie Kalman

Dedicated by Robin Johnson
For Granny Lil, who tickles the ivories and touches our hearts

**Author and
Editor-in-Chief**
Bobbie Kalman

Editors
Reagan Miller
Robin Johnson

Photo research
Crystal Sikkens

Production coordinator
Katherine Kantor

Design
Bobbie Kalman
Katherine Kantor
Samantha Crabtree (cover)

Photographs
All images © Shutterstock.com except:
Bobbie Kalman taken at Dolphin Quest Hawaii
    at the Kahala Mandarin Oriental Hawaii:
        page 23 (bottom left)
Comstock: pages 18 (honey), 19 (ice-cream sundae)
Corel: page 22
Photodisc: pages 19 (nuts), 32 (mouse)

Library and Archives Canada Cataloguing in Publication

Kalman, Bobbie, 1947-
    How does it feel? / Bobbie Kalman.

(Looking at nature)
Includes index.
ISBN 978-0-7787-3314-0 (bound).--ISBN 978-0-7787-3334-8 (pbk.)

    1. Touch--Juvenile literature. 2. Nature--Juvenile literature.
I. Title. II. Series: Looking at nature (St. Catharines, Ont.)

QP451.K34 2007   j508   C2007-904276-7

Library of Congress Cataloging-in-Publication Data

Kalman, Bobbie.
    How does it feel? / Bobbie Kalman.
        p. cm. -- (Looking at nature)
    Includes index.
    ISBN-13: 978-0-7787-3314-0 (rlb)
    ISBN-10: 0-7787-3314-9 (rlb)
    ISBN-13: 978-0-7787-3334-8 (pb)
    ISBN-10: 0-7787-3334-3 (pb)
    1. Touch--Juvenile literature. 2. Nature--Juvenile literature. I. Title.
II. Series.

QP451.K35 2008
612.8'8--dc22
                                    2007027237

Crabtree Publishing Company

www.crabtreebooks.com   1-800-387-7650

Published in Canada
Crabtree Publishing
616 Welland Ave.
St. Catharines, Ontario
L2M 5V6

Published in the United States
Crabtree Publishing
PMB16A
350 Fifth Ave., Suite 3308
New York, NY 10118

Published in the United Kingdom
Crabtree Publishing
White Cross Mills
High Town, Lancaster
LA1 4XS

Published in Australia
Crabtree Publishing
386 Mt. Alexander Rd.
Ascot Vale (Melbourne)
VIC 3032

Contents

How does it feel?

We have five **senses**. Our senses help us learn about the world around us. We **see** with our eyes. We **smell** with our noses. We **taste** with our mouths and tongues. We **hear** with our ears. We **touch** things to feel what they are like. Our sense of touch is in our hands and skin. What is this hand feeling?

We feel the world around us with our skin. This girl is being splashed with water. Her skin can feel if the water is cold or hot. Do you think the water is hot or cold? Why do you think so?

5

Is it hard or soft?

Is a turtle's shell hard or soft?
A turtle's shell is hard. The hard
shell protects the turtle's body.

How do you think it
feels to touch this mouse?
Does the mouse feel
hard or soft? Which other
animals feel soft?

Yikes! Spikes!

How does it feel to touch something with needles or **spines**? Spines are **sharp** spikes on animals or plants.

Does this iguana find the cactus plant **prickly**?

8

"Ouch!" Is that what you say when you feel something sharp? How must this lizard feel? Have you ever picked up a hedgehog? How do you do it without hurting your hands?

9

Furry or hairy?

Are bunnies **furry** or **hairy**?

Are they **fluffy** or **fuzzy**?

Is their fur hard or soft?

Do you think these monkeys like how this cat feels? Why?

Is this spider furry or hairy?   Is a caterpillar fluffy or fuzzy?

Slimy and slippery

Some animals have **slimy** coats. Slimy coats feel **slippery** when you touch them. This slug has a slimy coat. It is covered in **mucus**. Your body makes mucus, too. When you have a cold, you have a lot of mucus in your nose.

Frogs have slimy skin, too. They feel slippery when you touch them. Mucus keeps their skin **moist**. Moist means slightly wet.

Snails are also slimy.

Rough and bumpy

This baby bear is climbing up a tree trunk. Is the tree trunk **rough** or **smooth**? How would it feel if you were climbing up this tree with bare legs? Would it feel **scratchy**? Does it feel different to the bear? Why?

This alligator is sitting on a log. Is the alligator furry like a dog? Is the alligator grumpy because its skin is so **lumpy** and **bumpy**?

Is a snake's skin bumpy or smooth? It is very smooth!

Smooth and silky

A beetle is sitting on a pink flower. Is the beetle's body rough? Is it bumpy? No, the beetle's body is very smooth. It is shiny, too! The flower behind the beetle looks smooth and **silky**. Silky means thin and soft.

Which animal spins a web from silk? Did you guess that a spider does? This spider has made a big silky web. It has caught a fly in its web. Spiders eat flies and other insects.

Your mouth can tell

You use your fingers to feel food, but you also use your mouth. Your tongue can feel if food is cold or hot, sour or sweet, hard or soft. It can also tell you more about food. Look at the box below. It has some words about food. Find the picture of the food that matches each word or words.

1. cold and wet
2. thick and smooth
3. hard and sour
4. crunchy
5. sweet and sticky
6. lumpy and mushy
7. icy and creamy

apple

honey

nuts

mashed potatoes

smoothie

milk

ice cream sundae

Answers:

1. milk
2. smoothie
3. apple
4. nuts
5. honey
6. mashed potatoes
7. ice cream sundae

What is texture?

Texture is how something looks and feels. We can feel texture using our hands. We can see the texture of something with our eyes, too. We can see if something is bumpy or smooth. We can see if something is soft or hard. Sometimes we know how something feels. Sometimes we guess. Guess how this katydid's spines would feel to your fingers.

These clouds look like feathers. They are **feathery**. Do you think they feel like feathers? How do you think clouds would feel if you could touch them?

Under water

There are many textures under water, too. Talk about the texture of each of these underwater animals. Which one is prickly, bumpy, smooth, or hard?

sea turtle

dolphin

Which of these animals would you want to touch? Which would you not want to touch? Why?

sea urchin

Words to know and Index

furry
pages 10, 11, 15

fuzzy
pages 10, 11

hairy
pages 10, 11

hard
pages 6-7, 10, 18, 20, 22

spines

prickly
pages 8, 22

rough
pages 14, 16

slippery
pages 12-13

Other index words

bumpy pages 14, 15, 16, 20, 22

cold pages 5, 18

feathery page 21

fluffy pages 10, 11

hot pages 5, 18

senses page 4

sharp pages 8, 9

silky pages 16-17

slimy pages 12-13

texture pages 20, 22

wet pages 13, 18

smooth
pages 14, 15, 16, 18, 20, 22

soft
pages 6-7, 10, 16, 18, 20

touch
pages 4, 7, 8, 12, 13, 21, 22, 23

24

Printed in the U.S.A.